CHINESE
MIGRATIONS

Judith Kendra

Thomson Learning
New York

First published in the
United States in 1995 by
Thomson Learning
115 Fifth Avenue
New York, NY 10003

First published in Great Britain
in 1994 by Wayland (Publishers) Ltd.

Library of Congress Cataloging-in-Publication Data
Kendra, Judith.
Chinese migrations / Judith Kendra.
p. cm.—(Migrations)
"First published in Great Britain in 1994 by Wayland."
Includes bibliographical references and index.
ISBN 1-56847-239-0
1. China—Emigration and immigration—History—Juvenile literature. [1. China—Emigration and immigration—History.]
I. Title. II. Series.
JV8701.K46 1995
304.8'0951—dc20 94-29576

Printed in Italy

Books in the Migrations series

African Migrations
Chinese Migrations
Indian Migrations
Jewish Migrations

CONTENTS

Main Chinese Migrations
CANADA
BRITISH COLUMBIA
NORTH
Vancouver
AMERICA
Toronto
Sacramento
San Francisco
USA
New York
Washington DC
San Diego
Phoenix
ATLANTIC OCEAN
CENTRAL AMERICA
WEST INDIES
PACIFIC OCEAN
KEY
Areas of the world to which many Chinese people have migrated.

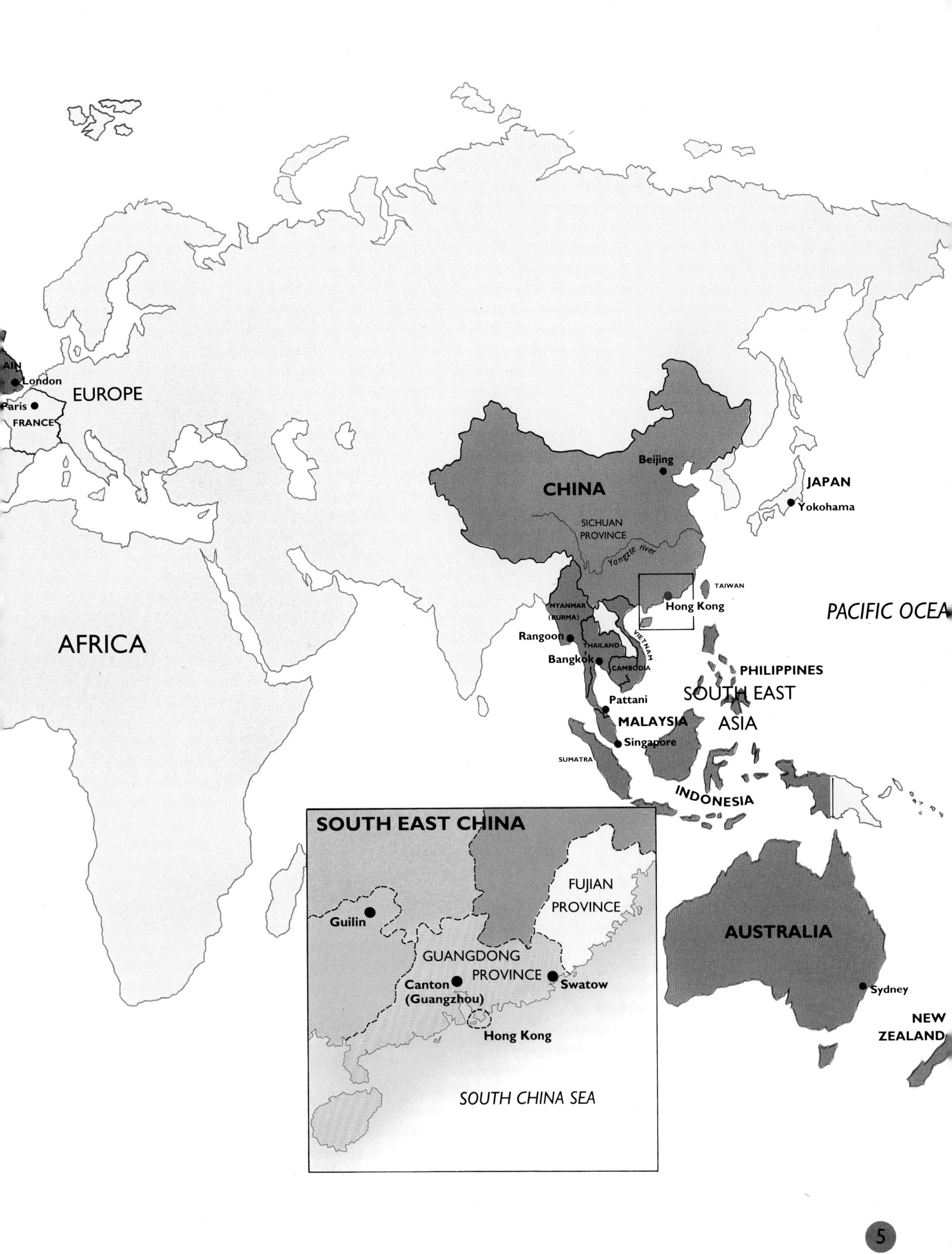

AIN
London
EUROPE
Paris
FRANCE
AFRICA
CHINA
Beijing
SICHUAN
PROVINCE
Yongzte river
JAPAN
Yokohama
TAIWAN
Hong Kong
PACIFIC OCEA
MYANMAR
(BURMA)
Rangoon
THAILAND
VIETNAM
Bangkok
CAMBODIA
PHILIPPINES
SOUTH EAST
ASIA
Pattani
MALAYSIA
Singapore
SUMATRA
INDONESIA
SOUTH EAST CHINA
FUJIAN
PROVINCE
Guilin
GUANGDONG
PROVINCE
Canton
(Guangzhou)
Swatow
Hong Kong
SOUTH CHINA SEA
AUSTRALIA
Sydney
NEW
ZEALAND

A new life

"My name is Meili Yip, though people here call me Mary. I'm ten years old and live in London with my parents. They came to Britain in 1984 from Hong Kong. My grandparents on my mother's side live in Canton [China], and those on my father's side live in Hong Kong. One of my uncles lives with his family in Vancouver [Canada] and another one lives in San Francisco. My sister is married and lives in Hong Kong."

This example shows you how migration from one country to another can affect a family, especially a Chinese one. But why do people migrate in the first place?

People migrate for a number of different reasons. Some leave their country for what they think are better opportunities elsewhere. Being tempted away like this is called a "pull" factor. Other people migrate because they are forced to do so. Reasons for these "push" factors can be such things as war, famine, floods, unemployment, or prejudice in the country they are leaving.

A Chinese migrant becomes an Australian citizen. In recent years, Australia has welcomed people from many Southeast Asian countries, including China.

What must it be like to leave your own country, possibly forever? Those who want to migrate will be looking forward to seeing new places, trying different foods, and finding different jobs. Some will be hoping to make their fortunes. They might dream of returning home one day wearing expensive clothes and bringing gifts for their relatives - just to show how successful they have become. Yet not all migrants will do well abroad. Some will barely make a living.

For those who do not want to migrate, the picture is a very different one. If they are being forced to leave because of war or discrimination, they may have to leave everything they possess behind. They may have a terrible boat trip or a very difficult, long walk before they reach a country where they are safe.

San Francisco's Chinatown. When the Chinese move abroad they try to support one another and re-create Chinese culture in their new countries.

In a new country, the first migrants try hard to keep up their language, religion, and the way of life they used to have in the old country. They try to make sure their children learn about that culture, as well as the new one. This becomes harder as more and more generations are born away from "home."

Most migrants will miss the friends and families they left behind. They will do their best to keep in contact, if this is possible. Some will hope to return to their homeland when they are older, if they are allowed to return and can afford to do so.

Chinese migration

The Chinese have a long and interesting history of migration. Tens of millions have left China over the centuries and have remained settled abroad. Most of them emigrated in the nineteenth and twentieth centuries, and most of them in recent years have gone to English-speaking parts of the globe.

A view from Moonhill, near Guilin, in southern China. Even if Chinese migrants live thousands of miles away in another country, they still feel attached to China.

Most Chinese migrants came from two provinces on the southern coast of China: Guangdong and Fujian (also called Kwangtung and Fukien). Fujian is about the same size as England, or the state of Ohio, and is mostly covered by mountains. Guangdong is larger and contains the important city of Guangzhou (also known as Canton), with Hong Kong not far away.

People speak a large number of different languages and dialects in the south of China (whereas most people in the north of China speak just one language, Mandarin). Those living in Fujian mostly speak Hokkien. Those living near Swatow in Guangdong speak Teochiu (also called Chaozhou or Chiuchow). Some in both provinces speak a form of Hakka.

Not surprisingly, those emigrating prefer to go to a place where the Chinese already living there speak the same dialect as they do. This is why, in the past, Hokkiens tended to sail to the Philippines, Singapore, Malaya (Malaysia), Indonesia, Burma (Myanmar), and southern Siam (Thailand). In contrast, Teochius often went to Bangkok (the capital of Thailand) and the Cantonese to the United States.

In Guangdong and Fujian provinces, a village is usually made up of just one big family, including aunts, uncles, and cousins, so they all have the same surname. They are proud to be able to trace back their family trees for generations. Family ties are important. When they emigrate they try to live close to one another and help one another as much as possible. This pattern has been clearly seen in some cities in the United States. For example, for many years, most of the Chinese in Sacramento had the surname of Fong; most of those in San Diego were named Hom; and most of those in Phoenix were named Tang.

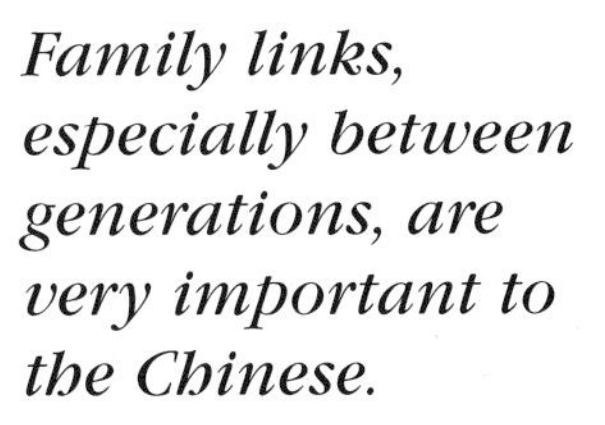

Family links, especially between generations, are very important to the Chinese.

No matter where he or she lives, a Chinese person has very strong feelings about the place his or her ancestors came from and where they are buried. Traditionally, the eldest son was expected to take care of his parents during their lifetimes. He was also expected to say special prayers in front of their graves (and the graves of their ancestors). Each family had a grave of its own, and if someone died away from home his or her body would be brought back to be buried there, if that was at all possible. These days, although these ideals about home remain, they are not often put into practice.

A shrine to ancestors in a Chinese temple. The plaques give their names and the photographs show their likenesses.

Mourners at a Chinese funeral in Malaysia. Performing the correct rituals at death is extremely important.

A well-known poem by Li Po shows the attachment of Chinese people to their homes:

> *So bright a gleam at the foot of my bed –*
> *Could there have been a frost already?*
> *Lifting myself to look, I see that it is moonlight.*
> *Lowering my head, I dream that I am home.*

Pirates and Traders

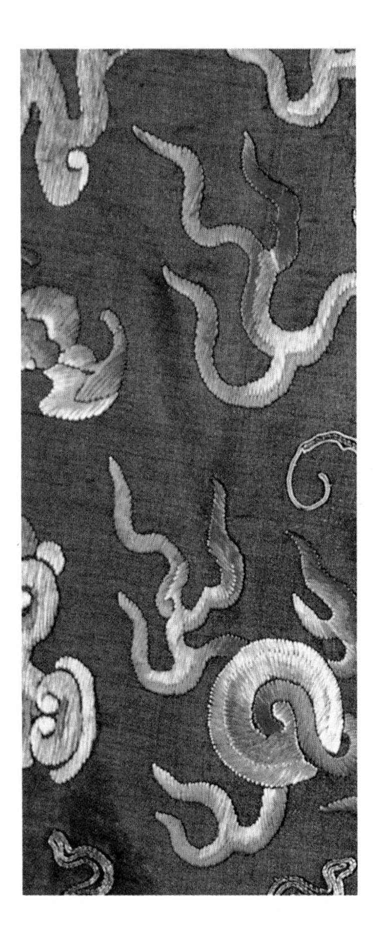

China is a nation with a rich and glorious past. This vast country has been the center of an incredible civilization that has been in continuous existence since at least 2000 B.C. The Chinese invented the arts of printing and tea making, as well as the manufacture of paper, porcelain, and silk. These things, among many, many others, were so ahead of their time that they seemed almost magical to outsiders. It was centuries before people in other countries were able to make silk or porcelain themselves, for example. It was not surprising, therefore, that foreigners wanted to trade with China. However, the Chinese, though very proud of their achievements, did not always want to trade with them.

The Chinese called their emperor "The Son of Heaven," because he was thought to be in a middle place, between heaven and people. As many ancient civilizations have felt about their rulers, the Chinese believed their emperor was the most important ruler of "all under heaven," or the whole world. Therefore, they divided the earth's peoples into Chinese and "barbarians," or those living in other countries who were not yet lucky enough to be ruled by The Son of Heaven.

A painting of the eighteenth-century Chinese emperor Kein-Lung.

Europeans approaching important Chinese people. Barbarians were expected to kneel in front of the emperor.

Barbarians were allowed to come to the imperial court to ask for special trading or political favors, as long as they brought presents (or tribute) for the emperors. Ordinary Chinese people, however, were not fully allowed to trade with foreigners until 1683, and going abroad was frowned on by the emperors until the end of the nineteenth century. There were many laws to keep them from doing so, like this one in 1799:

> *All officers of government, soldiers, and private citizens, who clandestinely [secretly] proceed to sea to trade, or who [go] to foreign islands for the purpose of inhabiting and cultivating the same, shall...suffer death by being beheaded.*

However, there were still many people who disobeyed the emperors by sailing away in their junks (Chinese boats) to Southeast Asia to try to make their fortunes. Throughout the fifteenth and sixteenth centuries, for example, these seamen called at the ports of such countries now known as Thailand, Malaysia, Taiwan, the Philippines, Indonesia, and Vietnam. Some of these traders settled in the foreign countries they visited and others became pirates.

A CHINESE PIRATE

Lin Tao-ch'ien was one of the most wanted outlaws of the South China Seas in the sixteenth century. He, together with a band of 2,000 men, escaped from Fujian province and sailed to Siam (now called Thailand). These men formed the center of a Chinese settlement at the port of Pattani. Here, they schemed and plotted how to raid not only the coasts of Southeast Asia, but also that of China itself. Eventually, Lin married the daughter of a local chieftain and ruled over a part of Malaya (now Malaysia) himself. [1]

From the sixteenth to the nineteenth centuries the Dutch, Portuguese, French, and British were looking for trading opportunities outside their own countries. They took control of different parts of the world, including parts of Asia, and called these places their empires. As these empires expanded, there were possibilities for many people to make money within them. These possibilities were pull factors for adventurous Chinese people. Wherever tin was being mined, tobacco or sugar being planted, rubber being tapped, or pepper being cultivated, the chances were that there would be Chinese people working to earn a living.

Chinese pirate junks (the large boats) being attacked in the Opium War, 1849.

During the nineteenth century, the British began selling large quantities of the drug opium to people in China. People became addicted to it very easily, so they spent large amounts of money on it, damaged their health, and were not always able to work. This brought hardship to many people.

An opium den where people came to take the drug in Shanghai, 1910.

The opium trade, although it was against the law, made much money for the British and paid for the legal trade they hoped to expand in the country. In 1840, to enforce their position, the British started a war with China, later called the First Opium War.

China lost the war, and so agreed to allow the British to occupy the island of Hong Kong and to allow foreigners to trade in five of the ports along its southern coast. Gradually the French and the Americans were given the same rights to trade with China.

The opening of the ports brought many foreign ships to China and far more possibilities of trade than ever before. This, in turn, caused many Chinese to move from their inland villages to the coast in search of work. From there, thousands and thousands sailed all over the world, migrating for better opportunities and a more stable place to live.

Chinese people traveled to Southeast Asia as well as to Africa, North, Central, and South America, the Caribbean, Great Britain, and many other places far away from their homeland. They lived not just in the coastal regions and the capital cities but also deep in the heart of their new countries.

They first went to Great Britain, for example, in the ships owned by the East India Company, which traded in Asia. Mostly seamen, they settled in London, Liverpool, Cardiff, Bristol, and Glasgow. In 1851, there were only 78 Chinese people in the country. Twenty years later, there were 202. By 1881 this number had increased to 665 (mostly because several shipping companies in Liverpool had started trading with China). By 1911, there were 1,319. Generally, they earned their livings by running laundries, stores, restaurants, and lodging houses for Chinese sailors.

Chinese migrants on a ship bound for the United States in 1884. The first migrants were always men: women joined the men only when they were settled in the new country.

AW BOON HAW: THE TIGER BALM KING

Named after the tiger (*haw*), Aw Boon Haw was born in 1882 in Burma (now Myanmar) to which his father had migrated from Fujian province in southern China. Aw Boon Haw and his brother inherited their father's herbalist shop, and in 1926 they moved to Singapore.

Here, Aw Boon Haw began to make and sell a strong-smelling ointment. It was called Tiger Balm and was supposed to be able to cure almost any ailment. The recipe was a secret but many people believed that it contained parts of a ground-up tiger. It has sold extremely well for years throughout Southeast Asia, making a fortune for Aw Boon Haw. It can also be bought in some Western countries today.

Tiger Balm can still be bought in many countries today.

Aw Boon Haw used the sign of the tiger on many things. For example, the car he owned looked like a tiger. Its headlights were the eyes, and the horn roared like a wild beast. The body was painted in black, orange, and white stripes. Everyone knew when its owner was on the move.

With his fabulous fortune, Aw Boon Haw also made the Tiger Balm Gardens in Singapore. These were somewhat like an early version of Disneyland with very brightly colored statues telling vivid stories of murders, myths, and legends. There were figures bleeding pints of painted blood, concrete kangaroos, women with chickens' heads, and other extraordinary things to see. [2]

Hard Labor

During the nineteenth century, many Chinese left their homeland because they were forced to do so. One of those push factors was a population explosion in China. Because there were too many people, it became very difficult for some to find enough to eat, to get work, and to take care of their families. Many left to seek their fortunes elsewhere.

Another push factor was the Taiping Rebellion, which took place between 1850 and 1864. This uprising, against the authority of the emperor, caused tremendous damage inside China: more than six hundred cities were destroyed and many thousands of people moved south and then fled abroad to escape the fighting.

Beggars in Beijing in about 1860. Poverty caused many people to try their luck in other countries.

Two methods of emigration became especially well known. One was the credit-ticket system, also known as free emigration. This was a way of receiving a free passage on board ship. If you could not afford the fare you were given a piece of paper, or a "ticket." This showed your name, age, where you had come from, and where you were going. When you arrived at your destination, the cost of your passage was paid by a friend, relative, or your new employer until you could afford to pay that person back. Chinese people who journeyed to Australia, Thailand, Singapore, Malaysia, and North America often used this system.

Another form of emigration was the "coolie," or indentured-labor, system. *Coolie* is believed to come from the Chinese word *ku-li*, meaning hard strength, and was applied to the thousands of men who were given contracts. Their contracts stated that they had agreed to work for someone abroad for a fixed number of years. Contract laborers were sent out from China to places throughout the world from 1845 on.

Sometimes, a man might have been down on his luck. He might have owed money, been a prisoner, or been starving. This sort of person could have been easily persuaded, or even tricked, into becoming a coolie. Once he had signed the contract and arrived in his new country, he became virtually the slave of his new master, just as Africans had been slaves before him. In fact, Chinese coolies often took the place of African slaves as cheap workers in the different European empires. And sometimes they were treated just as badly.

Chinese laborers were often treated like slaves by their new masters. Their work was hard, and it was many years until they were free again.

Coolies had to endure appalling conditions on the ships that took them to their new countries. These ships were almost always extremely overcrowded and their human cargo was often kept chained up in case of rebellion, or mutiny. A ship that was meant to carry 300 men might have 600 in its hold. The journeys were so terrible that, in the 1850s, as many as 15 to 45 percent of coolies died on their way to the Western Hemisphere.

Golden opportunities

Stories of making a fortune from discovering gold were common in the middle of the nineteenth century. Chinese migrants, along with other hopeful people from all over the world, rushed to look for gold in California, British Columbia, Australia, and New Zealand in particular.

Chinese miners panning for gold in the California goldfields, mid-nineteenth century.

Thousands of gold prospectors flocked to the West Coast. In 1852 alone, 20,000 Chinese passed through San Francisco on their way to the goldfields. For a time, there was so much work to be done in California and so few people to do it that prices were very high. Some miners found it cheaper to send their dirty clothes all the way back to Hong Kong to be laundered than to have them cleaned locally.

Thousands of credit-ticket emigrants left the area of the Pearl River Delta in southern China to look for gold in Australia. As many as 11,500 went to Victoria in 1855 and 12,500 to New South Wales in 1858. Sometimes, though, the local people did not like having so many newcomers arriving in their neighborhoods.

Chinese workers were often thrown out of Australian gold-mining camps by other miners.

When the U.S. railroads were finished, many Chinese laborers stayed and turned to other work.

Fights, some of them racist ones, broke out. In 1861, a thousand white miners in Lambing Flat in Australia went to attack the Chinese migrants among them. They marched behind a band, shouting as they went:

> *Rule Britannia! Britannia rules the waves!*
> *No more Chinamen shall land in New South Wales!*

Back in the United States, when gold began to run out, the Chinese became involved in making the new railroads. It took most of the 1860s to lay a track all the way across the continent, through mountains and desert, and the Chinese provided much of the labor to build it. It was such hard work that many Chinese lost their lives in the attempt. The same thing happened in Canada. In 1870, a newspaper reported that the bones of 1,200 railroad workers (weighing almost 10 tons) were shipped back to China for burial.

Wartime

Not many people know that the Chinese also took part in World War I on the side of the western Allies. At first, they were employed in Europe by the British and French. They helped in the factories, on the railroads, in the dockyards, and in other places. As a result, more French and British men were free to go to the front lines and fight.

When China entered the war in August 1917, however, the Chinese became involved on the battlefields themselves. They buried casualties, dug trenches, and took on other duties. Many were killed and some were buried on the French coast. The largest cemetery for Chinese is at Noyelles-sur-Mer in northwest France. It contains 838 graves.

During World War II, many U.S. and Canadian Chinese served in the armies of these two countries in their fight against Japan.

Needed, wanted, or hated?

For centuries, the Chinese living abroad have been sending money home. They have done this not only to help their families still living in China but also for business reasons. Over the years, these remittances have helped many people inside China. They have also helped the country as a whole. Between 1929 and 1941, for example, Chinese people living overseas sent back as much as $100 million every year.

A decorative arch, built by the Chinese community in Singapore to celebrate a British royal visit in 1922.

During various times in its history, the Chinese government made a special effort to look after Chinese people living abroad. This was partly to keep them loyal to China and partly to keep the remittances coming. From about 1920, therefore, schoolteachers were sent from China to teach children of the Chinese communities in Southeast Asia. The children learned about Chinese culture and also how to speak the Mandarin language. In this way, they continued to feel close to China. Yet this sometimes made them unpopular in their adopted countries because they seemed to care more for their old country than for their new one.

Fighting the Japanese in the streets of Shanghai, 1932. Although they lived thousands of miles away, many Chinese sent money to help the Chinese government defeat the Japanese.

When the Japanese army invaded China in 1937, the Chinese living abroad sent large sums of money to help the Chinese government. Later, when the Japanese invaded the countries of Southeast Asia, it was the Chinese living in them who often fought the hardest. This was especially true in Malaya where, in the 1930s, about 40 percent of the population was Chinese.

After the Japanese were defeated in Malaya, there was another period of fighting called the Malayan Emergency. During this new struggle in the 1950s, the Chinese were involved in fighting the British, who were ruling Malaya at the time. Eventually the British won, and, between 1950 and 1952, they sent nearly 10,000 Chinese people back to China.

China accepted these refugees. However, from the 1950s on, China generally encouraged the Chinese people abroad to think of themselves as part of their adopted countries rather than as Chinese nationals who happened to be living in different countries.

CLOTHING IN CHINA

The illustration below was made by Stanley L. Wood (1866–1928) for a book called *Peoples of the World* in 1896. It depicts a Westerner's idea of how the Chinese looked and dressed at the time.

China is well known for its silk, which was worn by men and women of high social stature. Often, patterns were embroidered on the front and back of their ankle-length coats. The patterns would instantly show the wearer's social status. Civil servants wore bird designs, and soldiers and sailors wore wild animal designs. Princes and ministers wore oval patterns, while mandarins wore square patterns. Their wives wore designs similar to those of their husbands.

Ordinary citizens wore long pants that flared at the bottom and a short robe or jacket. These were usually made of cotton; silk and other fine fabrics were only for the wealthy.

The color of clothing was also significant. Blue was the cheapest dye, so it was usually worn by the poor. Yellow could be worn only by the upper classes. Red, a symbol of luck and happiness, was worn by brides, while white was the color of mourning.

After the Communist revolution in 1949, people throughout China wore uniforms of plain working clothes. Traditional silk clothing was considered a decadent luxury of a class that no longer existed.

Indonesian youths breaking into the Chinese embassy in Indonesia's capital, Jakarta, in 1967. They attacked Chinese diplomats, burned papers, and wrecked the buildings.

During the 1950s, 1960s, and 1970s, the Chinese had mixed fortunes in Southeast Asia. In some countries, they seemed to be needed and wanted. This was because they were often very good at business or were prepared to do jobs that other people did not want to do. In other countries, though, they were hated. One reason was because they seemed to be loyal to the Communist government in China, and this government was often unpopular abroad. Another reason was because they seemed to be making much more money than other people in the country and were sending some of it out of the country. Sometimes the Chinese were hated for no other reason than because they were Chinese.

During the years after World War II, there was hardly a country in Southeast Asia where there was not discrimination against the Chinese. This brought a great deal of hardship to the Chinese communities in the area. For example, when the Khmer Rouge Communists took control of the capital of Cambodia in 1975, an estimated 200,000 ethnic Chinese died from starvation, disease, and executions. The Khmer Rouge specifically targeted the Chinese because they believed them to be rich. As a result, about half the Chinese population in the country died.

A temple in Cambodia where the Khmer Rouge killed many people. It is now a museum.

Another country that has a record of violence against the Chinese is Indonesia. It has been said that in no other place have more Chinese been killed or wounded, run away, or been chased away and been more insecure than in Indonesia. In 1966, hundreds of Chinese were killed in Sumatra (one of the islands of Indonesia). Their houses and stores were looted and slogans like this were written on the walls:

> *Drive out the Chinese now. You will be beheaded if you don't leave.*

In other countries, such as Malaya, the Chinese faced economic discrimination. When the British left the country in 1957, the Malays held political power and the Chinese held economic power (even though the Chinese made up only one-third of the population). In order to break the influence of the Chinese, the government gave the Malays special access to education, jobs, and other parts of the economic life of the country. The Chinese still have considerable economic power in Malaya, but small and medium-sized Chinese businesses are having a difficult time.

An injured man is helped by soldiers after being hurt during anti-Chinese riots in Jakarta, 1967.

Vietnamese boat people sailing into Hong Kong harbor after a hard journey. The government placed them in overcrowded camps where many had to stay for several years.

In Vietnam, government policies that discriminated against the Chinese caused an estimated 430,000 to 466,000 ethnic Chinese to flee the country between 1975 and 1979. Most could take none of their belongings with them, and they had no choice but to set out to sea in tiny boats in an effort to escape. They tried to reach China, Hong Kong, and other places in Southeast Asia, but thousands never survived the terrible journey. This was because other countries in the area (such as Thailand and Malaysia) did not want to receive the refugees. If they caught them arriving on a beach, they would tow them right back out to sea, to face another ordeal by storm, starvation, and pirate fishermen. The fishermen could be especially ruthless toward them:

> *The refugees are robbed, raped, or rescued, or all three... Most of them have some money, an old ten-dollar bill in a shoe or a trouser cuff... However, some of them have no money and that's what the fishermen can't believe. Sometimes the refugees come in [to the shore] naked.* [3]

A REFUGEE'S STORY

Mr. Ngoc, now almost 80 and living in London, had to escape from Vietnam by boat. "In China, I was a teacher of Chinese literature, but I escaped because of the Japanese invasion [in 1937]. I was only twenty-three... I went to Hanoi [North Vietnam] and became a journalist. I worked as an editor for twenty years... Under the Communist regime in Vietnam, I lost my freedom of speech and lived in extreme poverty. We all wanted to leave but there was no way through the usual channels. We knew it would be very dangerous to go by boat into those strong seas...

"One April, we left Vietnam by boat and drifted for several days before we arrived at Bei Hai [on the coast of China]. We repaired our boat and stocked up with food and fuel. We arrived in Hong Kong at the end of May. We went into a refugee camp and lived there for one year.

"I only considered going to the English-speaking countries because I'd learned a bit of English when I was young and I knew English was an international language. In April 1980 we came to Britain to settle." [4]

Thousands of Chinese who left Vietnam were put into prisonlike camps in Hong Kong.

Chinese People Today

Today Chinese migrant families can be spread all over the world. As more and more generations are born outside of China, it is inevitable that they will move to countries for all sorts of different reasons. Even a first-generation migrant does not necessarily remain in the same place for the rest of his or her life. He or she may migrate several times. Or, someone may move to one country for only a few years and then return home. Lili Chau, now working in a store in London's Chinatown, says this:

"I came to Great Britain three years ago as a student, especially to learn English. It's very difficult to learn English properly in China, you see, and since it's the number one international language, I think it's important to be able to speak it well.

"I'll stay here for four more years, because that's the amount of time I think it will take me to become properly fluent. Then I'll return to China where I hope I'll get a really good job. I have no relatives in England – they are all in China."

The Tiananmen Square massacre took place soon after this student protest in Beijing, May 1989.

These are some other typical life stories:

Mr. Phuong was once a fisherman in Vietnam. He escaped to Hong Kong in 1979 and then moved to Canada in 1984. Now living in Toronto, he works as a waiter in a Chinese restaurant.

Mr. Tan used to be a street vendor in Indonesia but fled from anti-Chinese riots in 1974. He traveled first to Hong Kong and then migrated again to Australia in 1987. Today, he and his family run a take-out food business in Sydney's Chinatown.

Many people - not just Chinese - come to shop in Chinese grocery stores.

Wang Dewei (who now calls himself David Wang) left China in 1989 after the demonstrations in Tiananmen Square in Beijing. (These protests, calling for more democracy in China, were brutally put down by the government, killing many people.) Wang went to the United States, where he was offered a place to study at the University of California. Once he has finished his courses, he hopes to get a job in New York - or maybe London or Singapore.

Today, many migrant Chinese feel more "rooted," or settled, abroad than they did 50 or 60 years ago. Although they will always have very strong ties to their ancestral home, they do not necessarily want to return there. Nowadays, a Chinese couple living in Hong Kong might actually wish to retire in Vancouver, for example, to have a quieter life.

Hong Kong

Chinese people have been flowing in and out of Hong Kong ever since the island was leased to Great Britain in 1842. Seven out of ten of its inhabitants have come from mainland China or have a parent who did. The population is also made up of many people who fled from persecution in other parts of Southeast Asia.

(Right) Hong Kong has grown massively since the British took it over in 1842. It is now a major world center for finance and Chinese culture.

Since the 1950s, Hong Kong has been a very successful commercial center. Many people have become very wealthy there and, on average, Hong Kong Chinese are 35 times richer than their relatives on mainland China.

Most of the Chinese videos and magazines in this shop in Sydney were made in Hong Kong.

Hong Kong creates fashions for Chinese living abroad. Most Chinese films and videos are made in Hong Kong and exported to Chinese communities around the world. Chinese newspapers in different capital cities all mention what is happening in Hong Kong (and China), as well as what is going on in their own countries.

However, the British lease on Hong Kong expires in 1997, and it will be given back to China. Many people believe that it will no longer be a good place in which to live and work. This is why many thousands of Chinese are now migrating from Hong Kong every year. Between 1986 and 1989, 5.7 million Chinese left for Canada, the United States, Australia, and England.

CHINESE BUSINESS PEOPLE TODAY

Sally Aw is one of Aw Boon Haw's daughters. When he died in 1954, she inherited one of the newspapers that he owned, the *Sing Tao Daily*. It was not long before she had made it the center of the largest newspaper empire in Hong Kong. The paper now sells editions in San Francisco, New York, London, Sydney, Toronto, and Vancouver. Sally Aw has been made an Officer of the British Empire and was the first woman to be elected as Chairman of the International Press Institute.

Mr. Li, a self-made billionaire, has been called "the man with the golden touch."

Another well-known Chinese business person is Li Ka-shing, one of the richest men in the world. However, he was not always a billionaire. Born in southern China, he arrived as a refugee in Hong Kong in 1940, at the age of twelve.

Two years later his father died, and Li Ka-shing had to leave school to take care of his family. He went to work in a factory. Gradually, he became a salesman, a manager, and then, at 22, he started his own company. Over the years, this business has turned into an empire that includes supermarkets, property, oil companies, and shares in newspaper and book publishing companies worldwide. [5]

Chinese people in Great Britain

The Chinese living in Great Britain come mostly from Hong Kong (though some are from Vietnam, Singapore, Malaysia, and China). Chinese men started arriving in large numbers in the 1950s because they could no longer make a living from farming and because Britain needed more labor during that period. (They migrated because of both push and pull factors.) Then, in the 1960s and 1970s, their wives and children migrated to join them. By 1981, over 25 percent of the Chinese in Britain had been born in the country and, by 1985, there were an estimated 122,000 in the community.

The Chinese quickly saw opportunities in the catering trade, and today about 80 percent of them make a living from businesses such as restaurants, take-out restaurants, and supermarkets. Whereas in the 1950s there was only a handful of Chinese restaurants in Great Britain, by the mid-1980s there were about 7,000 of them.

Many Chinese families have members living all over the world.

The family group is still very important to the Chinese living abroad. The father is the leader of the family and he and his wife do their best to ensure that their children do not lose their customs, beliefs, or language. If a family has difficulties, it will call on the support of close relatives and friends first of all before asking for help from non-Chinese people and government officials.

By establishing themselves so strongly in the catering trade in Britain, the Chinese play a part in British society that is appreciated by non-Chinese people. However, life is not always easy for them. About 70 percent of the first-generation immigrants are unable to speak English. Also, in 1984, it was found that only 52 percent of Chinese pupils in secondary schools were fluent in English. These language problems cause difficulties in communication, in passing exams, and in getting good jobs. Also, because they have to work such long hours in the restaurants and stores, there is not much time or opportunity to improve their English. Sometimes, the British are not especially friendly toward them, either.

Chinese restaurants are found all over the world.

Kim, a Chinese worker in a take-out restaurant in South London, explains:

"I came here from Hong Kong three years ago, and then my sister joined me shortly afterward. I work from 5 p.m. to 1 a.m., so I have the days free.

"I'd like to get to know British people my age but it's not always easy for us to understand each other – and sometimes they don't seem very interested in trying, to be honest. My sister and I don't have any other family here so we do a lot together. We could go into Chinatown in central London, but although there are Chinese people there, we don't know any of them either. It's nice here, but sometimes it's a little lonely."

JUNG CHANG AND AMY TAN

Jung Chang is the author of *Wild Swans*, a bestselling book about the lives of her grandmother, her mother, and herself in China. Not only is it an unforgettable story of three women, but it also gives a fascinating picture of the enormous changes that have occurred in China during this century.

Jung Chang receiving an award in London for her book Wild Swans.

Jung Chang was born in Szechwan Province in China in 1952. She left the country in 1978 to study English in England. She now lives in London.

Amy Tan was born in California, also in 1952, several years after her parents emigrated to the United States. Her first novel, *The Joy Luck Club*, was published in 1989. It is based on stories told by Tan's mother about her life in China, and about the relationship between women born in the U.S. to Chinese parents and their mothers. The book has been extremely successful and has been made into a movie.

Amy Tan says that, like many American-born Chinese, she has had some difficulties in understanding the parts of her that are Chinese and the parts that are American.

Amy Tan is well known for her books about Chinese Americans.

Chinese in the United States, Canada, and Australia

An enormous number of Chinese migrants have entered the United States during the last thirty years. By 1985 there were four times more Chinese in the United States than there had been in 1960. There is now about one Chinese person for every hundred people in the United States.

Most of the recent Chinese migrants in the United States come from Taiwan, China, the countries of Southeast Asia, and Hong Kong. They do not appear to have as many difficulties learning English, which means they can make good use of educational opportunities.

Jenny Kee is a Chinese Australian who is now one of the country's most famous designers. In 1973 she opened a small shop in Sydney, stocking her colorful fabric and knitwear designs, which are often inspired by Australia's plants, animals, and Aboriginal culture. By the end of the 1970s, her clothes were not only selling well in Sydney, but were also beginning to be popular in other parts of Australia, too.

Chinese-Canadian children in Vancouver.

JENNY KEE

Her international breakthrough came in 1982 when Princess Diana was photographed wearing a Jenny Kee sweater. Then the well-known fashion designer Karl Lagerfeld used her textiles for his clothes. Soon, Kee's designs were being sold in New York, Paris, Milan, London, Los Angeles, and Tokyo. [6]

Jenny Kee, who lives and works in Sydney. The city has a large, and growing, Chinese community.

As a result, they find jobs in almost every area of work. Some have become famous, including Tsung-dao Lee, winner of the Nobel Prize; Yo-yo Ma, the well-known cellist; I. M. Pei, the architect who designed the glass pyramid in front of the Louvre in Paris; and Betty Bao Lord, the novelist.

In some Canadian cities the presence of Chinese people is much more noticeable than in U.S. cities. That is because nearly all the 600,000 Chinese in Canada live in Toronto and Vancouver. Although in Canada as a whole two out of every hundred people are Chinese, in Vancouver, one out of every five people is of Chinese background.

Chinese culture

A concentration of Chinese stores, offices, and residences is usually called Chinatown. Most of the large cities of the world, including New York, San Francisco, London, Paris, Toronto, Vancouver, Bangkok, Yokohama, and Sydney, have their own Chinatown.

New York's Chinatown started in 1844. Although it was estimated that by 1988 there were 300,000 ethnic Chinese living in the city, not all of them lived in Chinatown. However, it is an area where they can meet one another for shopping, entertainment, and business.

The ornamental gate to London's Chinatown.

Great Britain's largest Chinatown is in London and is comparatively new. It started to develop in 1965, when five Chinese restaurants opened on Gerrard Street. Soon, other Chinese businesses moved to join them.

Today, many nearby streets in the district of Soho are humming with Chinese life. Here, you can buy Chinese groceries, eat in Chinese restaurants, and buy books and newspapers written in Chinese languages. If you are having legal difficulties, you can go to the Chinese Community Centre on Gerrard Street and ask advice from an expert. At this center, you can also leave your young children in the play group or take classes in English. On Sunday mornings, you can go there just to meet and talk to other Chinese people.

Chinatowns reflect modern life in the local Chinese community. A person can learn a lot just by wandering around, going into the shops, trying some of the Chinese foods, listening to Chinese music, and so on. Chinatowns are also the places where festivals are held. The Chinese New Year, for example, is celebrated in Chinatowns with a colorful procession. Fireworks are set off, the streets are decorated, and many Chinese and non-Chinese come to the area to enjoy the fun.

Chinese New Year celebrations in Chinatown, Washington D.C. People of all nationalities come to enjoy the colorful festival.

Another interesting place worth visiting is a Chinese herbalist, or drugstore. Chinese medicine has been practiced for thousands of years and can be divided into two parts: acupuncture (inserting very fine needles into the body) and herbal therapy (the drinking of specific herbal teas). The aim is to cure the body by putting it back in balance.

An herbalist's shop in the suburbs of Sydney. The herbs are stored in the drawers and jars and are measured out when requested.

When someone who is feeling sick has visited a Chinese doctor, he or she takes the prescription to the herbalist. Inside, there is usually a wall of small wooden drawers, as well as many glass bottles and other containers. These are full of the different herbs that the patient will add to water and drink as a tea. The herbs are collected and dried in mainland China and come from indigenous flowers, plants, treebark, leaves, and other similar sources. The herbalist weighs out the correct amount of these dried plants, according to the prescription.

Chinese medicine is known to be particularly good for treating skin problems. The office of a particular herbalist practicing in London's Chinatown is visited by both Chinese and non-Chinese people, and there are always long lines of patients waiting to see her. She has become so well known for treating eczema that Western skin specialists in a nearby hospital would like to learn the secrets of her success.

As you walk around Chinatown, you will also see many Chinese restaurants. Food and cooking are of great importance to the Chinese, so it is natural that some migrants will become involved in the restaurant business in their new countries.

HOW TO USE CHOPSTICKS

Chopsticks were invented at least 3,000 years ago in China. If you are used to forks and knives, it will take some practice before you can use chopsticks easily. If you've never used them, try these instructions:

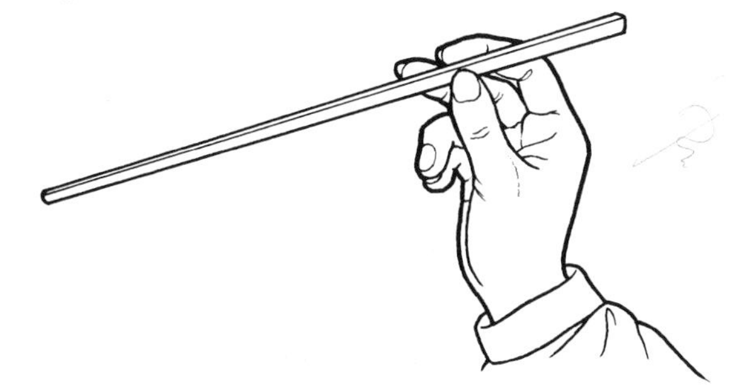

1. Hold one between your thumb, first, and second fingers, like a pencil. This chopstick is supposed to move like a lever.

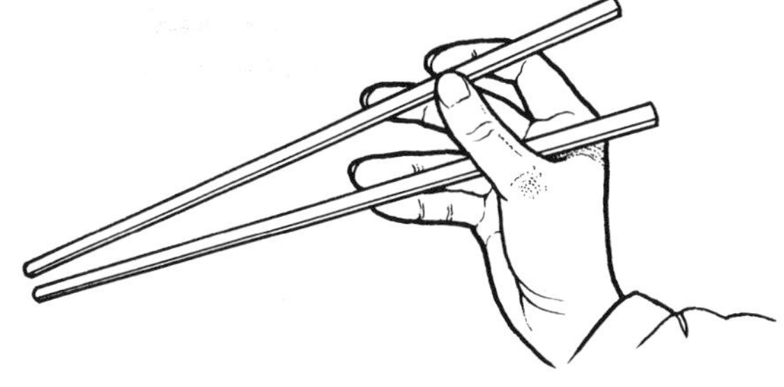

2. Take the other chopstick and place one end into the angle of your hand, between your thumb and first finger. Slide its other end between the ends of your third and fourth fingers. This chopstick is held steady. When used correctly, the chopsticks act as a kind of pincer.

Don't be surprised if it takes a little time to get used to chopsticks. You will be an expert when you can pick up three peanuts at once!

China is a huge country and different regions have different styles of cooking. In the north (which includes Beijing), dishes contain a lot of ginger and garlic, and the food is relatively heavy. In the east (around the Yangtze Delta) people eat a lot of fish and enjoy sweet dishes. Food from the west of China (including Szechwan) is likely to seem hot and is spiced with pepper and chilies. The cooking in the south, however, contains a great deal of fish and also includes many small snacks called dim sum. This southern food includes that from Canton. For many years the only Chinese cuisine eaten in the United States was Cantonese, but more recently highly seasoned Szechwan and Hunan cooking has become very popular.

Dim sum come in many shapes, sizes, and flavors. They include dumplings made with meat or fish, steamed buns, small crunchy rolls, and pieces of spicy meat.

The kind of cooking that is offered in Chinese restaurants depends on which part of China the chef is from. This principle also applies to other things you might see as you walk around Chinatown. Notice the different faces that people have - these may indicate whether they come originally from the north or the south of China. Notice, too, all the different kinds of books and papers at the newsstands, as well as the kinds of foods in the Chinese supermarkets. Try to find out if there is a temple nearby, and ask if you can look inside to see what is happening.

BIRD'S NEST SOUP

The Chinese consider bird's nests a great delicacy. Any old bird's nest will not do – it has to be the nest of a particular kind of small swift. It collects moss and feathers and other bits and pieces and sticks them (in the shape of nests) to the roof of caves with its saliva.

It is not surprising that by the time they reach stores around the world the nests are very expensive.

The nests are believed to give better health, particularly to men. They can be served in many different kinds of sweet or savory soups.

All these things show how much history and culture the Chinese person brings when coming to live in another country. If he or she is a first-generation migrant there will have been influences from either push or pull factors before leaving – and he or she may have lived in several different countries already. If a second- or third-generation Chinese, he or she may feel fully or only partly attached to the new country. Whatever the circumstances, the Chinese migrant helps to enrich the new country by sharing parts of the Chinese way of life.

Many Chinese people become well integrated into their new countries.

Glossary

Acupuncture The treatment of diseases by inserting very thin needles through the skin at carefully chosen places.

Ancestor A person from whom you are directly descended, usually farther back than a grandparent.

Communism A system of organizing people where land or housing is owned and controlled by a community or government rather than individuals, and each person works for the benefit of all.

Democracy A form of government where all the people have a say in what is decided, either directly or by choosing a representative.

Discrimination Treating a certain group of people badly because of negative feelings about their sex, skin color, language, religion, culture, or political beliefs.

Emigrate To leave one country in order to settle in another.

Empire A collection of peoples, territories, and countries under the rule of one person or government.

Ethnic Chinese A person who - even though he or she lives in a different country or speaks a different language - comes from the Chinese race.

Family tree A chart showing the relationships and different generations of one family.

Generation A group of people born at roughly the same time. For example, all the children in a family are in one generation. Their parents and their parents' brothers and sisters are in another generation.

Homeland The country in which a person was born.

Indentured labor Work agreed upon between a worker and a boss and sealed by a written contract.

Indigenous Coming from, or naturally occurring in, a country or region.

Khmer Rouge The Kampuchean (Cambodian) Communist party. Its brutal policies caused the deaths of thousands of people in Cambodia, especially the ethnic Chinese.

Lodging houses Places offering a temporary place to sleep and, sometimes, meals.

Looted Burgled from places that are unprotected after violent events, such as riots or war.

Lease An agreement where one person (or government) allows another to occupy land for a set period of time.

Mutiny Rebellion against authority, usually by soldiers or on board a ship.

Opium A drug made from the opium poppy.

Population explosion A rapid increase in the number of people living in a country or city.

Prejudice An opinion against, or in favor of, a person or thing, often made in ignorance. The word comes from "pre + judgment"; it is a judgment made before all the facts are known.

Race A general word for a group of people who share the same ancestors and may look similar. They may have the same type of hair, color of eyes and skin, and other physical characteristics.

Racist Belief that people's abilities and characteristics are influenced by the race they belong to.

Refugee Someone who has fled from danger, often from one country to another.

Remittance Money sent regularly, often through the mail.

Tribute Money paid by one country or ruler to another to pay for peace or for trading rights. Also, a present as a mark of respect.

Find out more

BOOKS

Bode, Janet. *New Kids on the Block: Oral Histories of Immigrant Teens.* America Past & Present. New York: Franklin Watts, 1989.

Daley, WIlliam. *The Chinese Americans.* The Peoples of North America. New York: Chelsea House, 1988.

Denny, Roz. *A Taste of China.* Food Around the World. New York: Thomson Learning, 1994.

Härkönen, Reijo. *The Children of China.* The World's Children. Minneapolis: Lerner Publications, 1990.

Lambert, David. *The World's Population.* Young Geographer. New York: Thomson Learning, 1993.

Lerner Geography Department. *China in Pictures.* Visual Geography Series. Minneapolis: Lerner Publications, 1989.

Marrin, Albert. *Mao Tse-Tung and His China.* New York: Viking Children's Books, 1989.

Mayberry, Jodine. *Chinese.* Recent American Immigrants. New York: Franklin Watts, 1990.

Ng, Franklin. *The Chinese American Struggle for Equality.* Discrimination. Vero Beach, FL: Rourke Corp., 1992.

Sherwin, Jane. *Human Rights.* World Issues. Vero Beach, FL: Rourke Corp., 1990.

Steel, Philip. *China.* World in View. Milwaukee: Raintree Steck-Vaughn, 1990.

Takaki, Ronald. *Ethnic Islands: The Emergence of Urban Chinese America.* The Asian American Experience. New York: Chelsea House, 1994.

Takaki, Ronald. *Journey to Gold Mountain: The Chinese in 19th Century America.* The Asian American Experience. New York: Chelsea House, 1994.

Waterlow, Julia. *The Ancient Chinese.* Look Into the Past. New York: Thomson Learning, 1994.

Wu, Dana Ying-Hui and Tung, Jeffrey Dao-Sheng. *The Chinese-American Experience*. Coming to America. Brookfield, CT: Millbrook Press, 1993.

MOVIES

Chinese Gods (1980)

Dim Sum: A Little Bit of Heart (1985)

Eat a Bowl of Tea (1989)

Empire of the Sun (1987)

The Good Earth (1937)

Iron & Silk (1991)

The Last Emperor (1987)

The Joy Luck Club (1993)

USEFUL ADDRESSES

China Institute in America
125 East 65th Street
New York, NY 10021

Chinese American Citizens Alliance
415 Bamboo Lane
Los Angeles, CA 90012

Chinese Historical Society of America
650 Commerical Street
San Francisco, CA 94111

Office of the President of Taiwan
Taipei, Taiwan
Republic of China

Office of the President of
the People's Republic of China
Beijing
People's Republic of China

Notes on sources

1 *Sons of the Yellow Emperor: Story of the Overseas Chinese* by Lynn Pan (Mandarin, London, 1991).
2 *ibid.*
3 *The Spectator*, London, June 30, 1979.
4 *Hackney Pensioners' Press*, London, date unknown.
5 Pan, *op. cit.*
6 *Made for Australia* by Judith Kendra (Harcourt Brace Jovanovich, Australia, 1990).

Index

Entries in **bold** indicate subjects shown in pictures as well as in the text.

PICTURE ACKNOWLEDGMENTS

Archiv fur Kunst und Geschichte, Berlin 11, 12, 14; Associated Press 25, 27; The Bettman Archive 19; Camera Press 7 (Joachim Messerschmidt), 11 top (F. Fischbeck), 21 top (F. Fischbeck), 28 (Chris Davies), 29 (Chris Davies), 40 (Nicholas Holt), 44 (F. Fischbeck); Chapel Studios 38; Eye Ubiquitous 6, 8 (Julia Waterlow), 10 (Simon Arnold), 26 (Tim Page), 32 (Matthew McKee), 33 (P. Thompson), 42 (Matthew McKee); Impact 31 (John Cole); Peter Newark's Historical Pictures 13, 15, 17 (bottom), 18, 20 (bottom), 23, 24; Photri Inc. 41 (Lisa Sardan; Rex Features (Sipa Press) 30-31; Robert Harding *contents page* (Adam Woolfitt), 9 (Adam Woolfitt), 17 (top), 36 (Adam Woolfitt), 45; Royal Commonwealth Society Collection 22; Topham Picture Source 20 (top), 34, 35, 37 (John Stillwell); Wayland (Z. Mukhida) *cover* and *title page*.